I0622860

WALKING HOME WITH LOVE

108 Messages to the Divine

Stever Dallmann PhD

Walking Home Press

Maui, Hawaii, USA

www.walkinghomepress.com

Copyright © 2023 Steven "Stever" Dallmann PhD

All rights reserved

No part of this publication may be reproduced in any form

without the written consent

of the publisher or author.

First edition: 2023

ISBN 9798989312429 (Paperback)

ISBN 9798989312436 (e-book)

Library of Congress Control Number: 2023947979

Table of Contents

INTRODUCTION

Thank you for opening this little journal.

These pages are a record of the words, tone, and heart of my personal messages to, and conversations with, the Divine. The writing here isn't meant to be poetry. I don't claim any ability to that fine craft. These are just the simple words I really used when talking with the Beloved. The poetic formatting is my attempt to give you a sense of the pace and flow of the messages.

One day, some years ago, I started writing down a few of these private messages, and sharing them, shyly, with others. I've been encouraged to share these even more. Thus, this small book.

My hope is that the essence of this offering is accessible to anyone, regardless of belief. Presence, Beloved, God, the Divine, the Mystery, Friend, the One, Love… there are so many names for that which is beyond words. I believe that we each have our own personal experiences of that Love. May we all be free to experience and express it as we choose, by any name that feels right for you.

My invitation to you is to explore these offerings softly and slowly, as if taking a walk, finding something interesting on the path, and picking it up to see what might be waiting inside for you.

My prayer is that you get a little something you can use from one or two of these offerings. Perhaps a smiling moment of positive glow. Perhaps a brief glimpse of the Light. Perhaps even a taste of the Love that is here for us all.

I

ONE

INSTRUMENTATION

It seems that You have given me a choice in life.

When I choose to make it all about me,
life feels so very heavy and burdensome.

When I choose to just play along,
offering myself to You as an instrument,
life flows through me.

The Saint Francis Prayer says:
"Make me an instrument of Your Peace."

Yes, please!
Make me an instrument
of Your Peace, Your Will, Your Grace, Your Love.

Maybe, though, not a celestial harp,
glowing with a halo of gold
but, for me, perhaps a kazoo!

Or, better yet,
make me a simple humble wooden flute,
waiting for your breath to flow through me,
so Your sweetness can pour out into the world,
like it does from the throat of a bird.

Every

Note

is for

You.

WAKING UP

Sweet

Sacred

Love

You are HERE!

WEAR IT

Every morning I meditate, pray,
brush my teeth, and get dressed.

Although I talk with You
and feel your Presence,
it can be challenging to hold that Love
consistently in my mind all day.

So, I wear it.

My morning prayers
are like getting dressed.
I consciously drape myself in the Love,
donning it like a shawl
or a lei
or a really comfy shirt.

And I don't take it off.

I wear Your Love in all its glory
Wrapped in my true essence and purpose.

Wherever I go,
Whatever I do,
Wherever my mind or moods go,
There is Love.

MAGIC

A big-eyed 6 year old asked me
"Are you still sick?"

"Nope" I replied with a grin
"I feel great!"

Eyes bigger, she exclaimed
"Wow! What happened?"

"Well, I just sang a prayer, went to bed,
and woke up well."

Knowingly, she nodded
"Yeah, that's how Love works.
It's magic."

SHARING

Today I read a few of these messages to a wonderful soul.

The notes feel so personal and simple,
something special between You and me,
that at times I think they should be left alone,
a private treasure hovering in time.

But on this sunny relaxed afternoon,
I shyly shared some of these offerings,
and it went well.

Later I laughed at the foolishness of keeping them to myself

As if
Your Love
and the free-flowing Joy I experience with You
is something to hide or possess.

As if
I can do anything but share
the Light that's already everywhere.

BOWL OF APPLES

Struggling with an issue,
wondering what I should do,
I found myself sitting in front of a fragrant bowl of apples.

Beautiful bundles of round red sweetness
Each one the same
Yet each one unique
Which one should I choose?

Each came from a tree
that blossomed and bore fruit.

Apples get picked.
Or they fall
and eventually wither away
leaving only the seeds.

Each seed ready to sprout another tree.

As I breathed in,
One apple fell from the bowl and rolled towards me.

I took a bite and got lost
in the flavor of the moment.

Embraced by the taste,
the nourishment,
the sweetness,
I felt Your Love -
So delicious!

What was the problem I was so concerned with?

Ah, it was solved by Love and a bowl of apples.

No need for struggle or worry -
The answers will ripen and roll forward at the perfect time.

BEING

After a brief morning prayer, I sit with You and say
"What should I do today?"

You say
"Let's skip the 'doing' and 'shoulding' and just be."

"Be Love."

Ahhhh, ok, that's the plan.

So I relax
and from that serenely spacious space
arises joy
and then
some excitement for my next action
which lovingly flows into the next action,
and the next,
and so on

as we dance through the day.

PULSE

Dear One,

Deciding to take my pulse
I placed fingers on my wrist
while repeating Your name
with every beat.

At first
the rhythm gradually speeded up
excited by the thought of You.

But instead of reaching a dramatic crescendo
the pace evened out
to an ever widening
steady
flow
of Love.

My heart is Yours

THE PAST

I used to think a lot about the distant past
often with feelings of regret, sadness and loss.

Now and then the thoughts would be accompanied
with shades of pride or joy or fond sentimentality,
but, always,
I was holding onto something
that tasted bitter sweet.

Now though,
hanging out with You,
if the past comes to mind
just one thing shines
as essential and true -

You were there.

II

TWO

DAYBREAK

What a stunning sunrise!

The night was cold and dark,
nightmares in the shadows.

But now,
as always,
here comes the daylight.

The sun,
an agent of Your vast Love,
radiates -
enlivening my heart,
warming my weary bones,
and filling my eyes with wonder.

Slowly I spread my arms -
Lifting my wings
to the beaming blessings
of another day.

Thank You!

WORDS

Sometimes You come to me on the wind,
in the scent of marigolds,
or through the morning song of a bird.

But today you are making yourself known to me through words.

As I read,
my eyes take in your flowing grace.
As I write,
I'm filled with wonderment at Your gift of creativity.

As I speak,
every sentence I utter,
every phrase I hear,
has Your glow
nestled within the bounty of language itself.

The miracle of ideas coming through a mind
and out into the world on a page or a breath is astounding.

Most amazing and precious to me
is that I get to talk with You like this,
and write it down.

In Your Presence, all words are the language of Love.

WHAT'S HAPPENING?

Beloved,

Sometimes my world gets busy and small, like today:
I was working on the computer,
thinking about a person that was rude to me,
and worrying about this and that.

Then a bird stopped by my window and sang for a moment -
just long enough to remind me to check in with You.

I smiled, took a deep breath, and said to myself,
"I wonder what God is up to today?"

I turned towards You, and was amazed by what I saw!

You are always doing something infinitely more interesting
than what my little mind stirs up on its own.

I spent the rest of the day working with You.

What a wonderful time we had!

THE LIFE PRESERVER

Thank you for the afternoon of swimming in the welcoming water!

I'm reminded of when I was 7 years old. We had a new swimming pool and I didn't know how to swim.

In fact to the adults I seemed troublesomely void of any natural athletic prowess or coordination.

So my parents insisted that I always put on a big orange life preserver to keep me from drowning.

Oh, how I loved being in the water!
I would swim with delight for hours on end.

One hot day my dad happened to pick up the big orange life preserver from where it sat on the sizzling concrete.
How heavy it was! He dropped it into the pool and it quickly sank to the bottom.

My preserver was waterlogged and had actually been a hindrance and threat to my safety.

Without the weighty baggage I instantly knew how to swim.
I was free to dance in the water from that day on.

Oh Lord, how many big orange life preservers have I or others insisted that we need in order to swim in your ocean of Love,
when in fact they were just weighing us down?

How delightful it is when the cautious restrictions
I clung to so desperately fall away and I'm free!

Free to swim in your infinite sea,
diving peacefully into the depths,
leaping gleefully though the waves
into the sparkling light!

You have graced me with the life of a dolphin.

MANY PATHS

Sitting serenely at a local cafe
on a peaceful morning
I somehow got into a conversation
with the tourist family at the next table
about Buddhism.

Then someone else nearby chimed in about Christianity.
Soon a local yogi came by with his views.
This continued and, before I knew it,
there had gathered a small spontaneous interfaith convention
around my little table and chai latte.

So many different paths
So many different experiences
So many opinions about You
and even discussions on whether or not You exist.

But
when I spoke of Love
everyone smiled.

From that perspective
they all seemed to know You well.

WHY

I asked the question.

I hear Your answer.

Ah, ok, so that's
Why I'm here:

To delve
ever deeper
into the mystery
into the Presence
into the Love.

Love
Love
Love

From there I serve.

THE CARVER

I watched as the strong and gentle Hawaiian man
carved the Koa wood.

His tools were sharp, hard, and rough –
capable of brutality.
But he used them so softly and skillfully
hat each cut or stroke
shaved away only the layers which had to go
in order to uncover
the beauty that was waiting majestically to be revealed.

The creative process was a delightful and delicate dance.
What emerged was an exquisite sculpture,
full of joy and grace.

So it is with You, the most skillful of artists.

With every one of our trials,
challenges, and lessons.

You are lovingly shaving, cutting, and sanding away –
removing everything that's in the way
of You and Your perfect creation.

Each of us is an expression of Your Love

SHOPPING

Dear One,

Where do I go
when I'm not consciously hanging out with You?

Shopping, mostly,
in one way or another,
for things I don't really need.

All I ever really need
is
You.

IN THE FIELD

I stood in the field alone
Light pouring onto me
and through me.

The birds chirping
and the infinitely grinning greenery saying
Yes! Come grow with us!

You speak to me
through all your vast creations.

Every leaf whispers your Love.

I just have to stop and listen.

III

THREE

SUNDAY MORNING

Walking through the quiet city streets
on an early Sunday morning
I stopped and asked:

"Where am I going?"

"Where are you?"

You said:

"I am here."

"Just keep walking, and wait for Grace."

The sun came up
shining on the trees and vibrant plants

Hopeful strands of grass
reached up through the concrete cracks.

I've never seen the streets more beautiful.

MEMO

I was dreaming of transitions
and a colorful metamorphosis -

My Soul in flight.

As I awoke there was a giant butterfly
resting on my bedroom window.

The early morning light
poured through those intricate wings,
shining directly into my eyes.

Your message was exquisite,
Your memo, perfectly poetic.

You are always Present -

in my dreams,
in my waking hours,

and in all the journeys
in between
and beyond.

Thank You for the truly angelic reminder!

CLOUDS

Watching the clouds, I learn how Your universe works.

Moisture, air, light, and wind currents gather together to play,
and a cloud is formed.

It may be faint and wispy, or round and fluffy like cotton,
or dark and heavy, pouring down on the earth.

But the cloud always fades away, disappears, or transforms -
just a temporary dance of the elements -
like thoughts,
moments,
and lifetimes.

Oh yes, the performance is very real:
Look at how dramatic that storm cloud is!
See how stunningly beautiful the colorful one is at sunset!

But I see no sense in holding on to any of them,
or in giving one a name,
or praying that it stays there forever.

You've taught me to just let them play,
and enjoy Your glorious artistry.

NANA

Feeling sick and tired today
reminds me of when I was a child
quiet and frail.

When I was 8 years old, my grandmother, Nana, came to visit.

She got up early every morning
to read holy scripture and inspirational stories.
While everyone slept, she and I read about and discussed…. You.

I would always be enlivened by the readings
and glow into the morning.

Throughout the day I would yearningly ask for more.
"Oh, honey, that's only for mornings and Sundays,"
Nana would say, as she sipped her peppermint schnapps.

Today, all these years later,
I get to snuggle – warm, comfy, and hopeful
with my pile of inspiring books and scriptures.

Ah, this weary sickness is a blessing!

Your Grace and Light reminding me once again that
You are Here.

Thank You.

IN THE SAND

At the ocean's edge
I wrote Your name in the sand.

I sat
watched
and
breathed in
Your Presence.

Then I saw Your name -
Not just where I'd written it
but on each and every tiny grain of sand!

Every particle of the Universe
Has Your name on it.

Every particle
vibrates
with
Your Love.

Walking home from the beach,
the sidewalk sang to me Your praises.

PERCENTAGES

My mind has a tendency to constantly calculate things,
just like the technology that surrounds me.

How much memory is left on my laptop?
What amount of money do I need for a vacation?
How long does it take to bake a pizza?
How much screen time is too much?

So I wondered:
how much time do I spend each day
focused
on
You?

What's the percentage?
What's the computation?

A wise person said that we only need to use
25% of our mental capacity for day to day functioning in this world.
All the rest,
75%, could be spent focused on You.

What a delightful and delicious calculation that is!
I will work joyfully and diligently on adjusting my percentages.

So that while
driving the car,
or paying my bills,
or washing the dishes,
most of my awareness can be hanging out with You.
Yay!

TRANSPLANTING

Here we are my Beloved,
on a sunny day,
as rich and marvelous as any festive holiday.

To celebrate, I'm transplanting a young, flowery Plumeria.

The stalk is only a foot high right now but,
with good soil and water,
it will reach up into the light,
and offer its exquisitely tropical blossoms,
their fragrance dancing in the air with pure joy.

In this process, with you at my side,
I too am transplanted -
into Now.

This place, this perfect time,
this lovely point in the winding road of my life -

You have graciously shown me the way
and carried me here,
just as I am carrying this plumeria.

Here I am, in this most glorious moment,
rooted in rich soil,
reaching up with all my leafiness,
into Your Light.

POSTCARDS

Sometimes,
when I get lost in Your Love,
I realize how truly heavenly
life can be.

From that place,
I scribble out my messages to You
on these little postcards,
as reminders of how to get there
and of how indescribably delicious it is
to
be
in
Your Presence.

BATHROOM FLOOR

Dear One,

What a radiantly delightful day this has been!

Each moment
full of life
and surrounded by Love.

How did I get here?

So many years ago
in my darkest hour
on the bathroom floor
sick, tired, toxic, dying.

I had to surrender
and stop trying to do it all myself.

I begged for help
and there You were.

IV

FOUR

PEEPING TOM

Sometimes, when I'm walking down the street
I look into people's eyes and I feel like a Peeping Tom!

It's not that I'm looking for anything
titillating
secret
or perverse.
I don't mean to offend.

I'm just looking for You.

You are always in there, somewhere,
but, usually, the blinds are drawn and the lights are out.

Sometimes, though, when I look into people's eyes,
You are right there
and it startles me!

All that deep bright knowing Presence,
suddenly smiling right back at me.

When I thought I was being stealthy and coy.

LITTLE MIRACLES

Last night I attached a thread to a small
clear
multifaceted
cut glass crystal
and hung it in front of my window.

It was a simple act
that felt
like a prayer.

This morning I opened the curtains and my room was flooded
with a flock
of delicate
bright
and brilliantly shimmering
little rainbows!

Once again, You remind me
that a tiny effort on my part
can open a wondrous portal
through which I can see
Your miracles
radiating into the world.

Wow.

POSSIBILITIES

Sometimes I sit in my chair
feeling stuck
wondering what I can do,
if anything.

Then,
by some miracle,
I remember
to take a breath
and pray - one way or another.

Then,
bam!
The lights come on.

You tell me
once again
that I am free.

Then
there We are
creating
serving
dancing
Loving
with glorious abandon!

When I connect
to the exhilarating energy of Your Love
All things are possible.

PILGRIMAGE

They say,
to get closer to You:
go to
India
Jerusalem
Mecca
or
the most desolate desert
or
the highest peak of the Himalayas.

For a short encounter,
there are churches
and temples.

Those places are so wonderful,
but:

My Beloved,
I don't want to be a spiritual tourist
trekking to visit You.

I want to be with You always.

Maybe, to get closer to You
I could go live on the banks of the Ganges
or
devote myself to an isolated monastery
or
spend the rest of my life in a sacred cave.

But even then
at some point
the journey
leads
within.

At some point
it's time to stop visiting You
and start being
in Your Presence
always and all ways.

Then we can journey to these amazing places together.

NOWHERE

Once, when I was a teenager,
the world felt so hard,
so painful,
that I just wanted out.

So I took my mom's old car and drove way outside the city,
taking left turns and right curves and country roads,
determined to get lost.

A farmer had left a gate open, so I drove into the pasture, over a slope, and
into the middle of a big field.

At last I was where I wanted to be - nowhere.

It was sunset.
With a deep breath I inhaled the late summer air
and I cried.

I cried until it was night -
and the darkness encircled me.

Then - a firefly!
and another,
and another,
and more,
and more,
until I was surrounded by little beams of light.

I lost myself in the wonder of the moment.

I looked up -
oh the stars!

I stood in awe
as You whispered faintly:
"This is who you are."
"Look at all the Light you're making!"

You used that little firefly to ignite my Soul -
lifting my heart and my eyes
to look up
at You.

I was ready to move forward and live my life.

To this day, I always remember:
It only takes one spark to Light up the dark.

IN FLIGHT

Ah, the wonders of this planet and Your creations!
It's a beautiful day for some air travel.

Interesting how so many of my fellow passengers
close their window shades quickly after take off.
They want a better view of the tiny screens in front of them.

I understand.
My mind, like theirs, is an active little child
in need of games and entertainment.

But my Soul…

My Soul likes the window shades open.

Through that portal I can see, and feel,
the vastness of Your planet
and witness this little spot in Your infinite universe.

As I allow myself to expand into that spaciousness,
my mind calms down.

You are here!

You say "Come fly with me!"

How could I possibly refuse.

REDWOODS

Deep in the forest I'm awed once again by your majesty.

What a glorious temple nature has created!
Every tree, every branch, every fiber
reaching up
in earnest prayer to you.

When it rains on this temple,
there emerges a rhythmic symphony.
Even after the rain has stopped
the water drops continue to fall from the trees
prolonging the hymn for hours.

Behind that melody, the chant of the creek emerges
louder and louder, running down the hill
to the stream
to the river
thrilled to be rushing back to your infinite ocean.

I hope that I can learn from these trees
how to reach for You
how to receive Your Grace
how to be so drenched in Your life-giving Love
that the droplets don't stop rolling off of me
until Your light shines down
and they rise as mist to greet You.

CLEANING HOUSE

At times, my thoughts and reactions
bounce around in my head
with such a circus of activity
that they seem important and real -
frantic performers kicking up a cloud of mental dust
so thick that I can't see anything else.

Once in a while, though,
the illusion clears just a bit,
allowing me to look around
and notice that it's time to clean house.

So I grab whatever tools I need
and start doing the simple task that's right in front of me.

As I wipe or sweep, my attention begins to focus.
The broom becomes a meditation tool.
The dust clears
and there I am
Present in the moment.

And there You are!
Grinning at me with
kind
soft
Loving
laughter
saying

Welcome home.

BIG GLASSES

At the cafe today
a visitor tried on my friend's new designer glasses
the ones with the great big lenses.
He said something fun and silly and we all laughed.

I sat down and started thinking about lenses, light, and vision.

Give me new eyes Lord!
Or perhaps just new big silly glasses,
Magical glasses designed exclusively for looking at You.

Then with my delightfully adjusted vision
You can guide me in all I do.

Everywhere I look
any way I turn
there will be You and Your Love.

Whatever I see,
may I see You in it.

Whatever I do,
may there be Love in it.

V

FIVE

THE PRIMARY COLOR

Your Love is like a most exquisite and radiant color!

The glorious glow weaves through the entire rainbow,
vibrating constantly in absolutely everything.

But this Divine hue is outside the spectrum
of normal human vision.

We can only see it
if
we use our hearts
as the lens
through which
we view the world.

ASSETS

Dear One,

Thank you for hanging out with me!

There were times
as a kid, as a teenager, and beyond
when I felt so alone.

I was odd, quirky, weird.

Little did I notice
that You were right there
with me
the whole time.

And it was my oddness, quirkiness, and weirdness
that, eventually, would lead me
to reach out for You
with total abandon.

Apparent "deficits" can become major assets
in Your light.

DATING

For so long I searched for someone to love and adore,
someone who would also love and adore me just as I am.

At work, on the street, in cafes and bars,
I anxiously watched and waited.

Where was my match made in heaven?

Meanwhile I started to get to know you better and better.
My prayers then were like first dates
tenuous and unsure, curious and excited.

Gradually you awakened my true heart
and now I am yours
forever madly lost in Love with You.

You - My divine Light.
My true Beloved.
My all and All.

Here you are!
At my side, loving me just as I am, no matter what.

When sadness or insecurity creep in,
You whisper in my ear:

"I am here."

"You are wonderful."

"Take my hand."

THE WORKPLACE

Dear One,

I'm thinking about that dog I had for so many years, Sully.
I loved her so much.

Whenever I would get ready to leave the house without her,
she would first become anxious, then her tail would go down,
her cuddly excitement shrinking in sadness.

I could barely manage to walk away, my heart yearning
to stay with the furry form of Unconditional Love,
or to take her with me.
But my work place wasn't dog friendly, so I left her behind.

It feels the same with You.
I do my morning prayers and practices.
Then the phone rings, the schedule and to-do lists pull on me.
I look back at the smoldering candle, my heart breaking from being pulled
away into the busy delusions of day-to-day life.

Today, though, it's different.
I've decided to strive harder to bring You with me.

Can You help me create a God friendly workplace?

Wherever I am, my workplace is my mind.
Maybe that bustling enterprise can lighten up
and give its wise approval to a new project:
The blossoming of a constant awareness of your Presence.

May I always have your Love on my mind.
I can no longer bear to leave You behind.

WAITING

Waiting for my friend,
she's late.

Dear One,
I never have to wait for You.

You are always here,
no appointment needed.

How sweet it is,
to sit on this bench
with Your Presence.

Now that You and I are hanging out,
my friend can take as long as she needs.

The wait is a blessing.

THE RESTART BUTTON

Almost anything can pull me off center.

A minor upset,
a big issue,
or just a grumpy mood,
and there I am
riding a broken bicycle in useless circles.

Gratefully,
my relationship with You has taught me
how to restart my day.

I can push that magic button any time.

All I have to do
is pause for a minute
to Pray,
Meditate,
Chant
or just think of You.

Then there I am
in Your Presence
and everything begins anew.

CLASSROOM

I've read so many holy books,
And books about holy books.
So much inspiration.
So many great souls pointing the way to you.

But today my Beloved
I put aside the books, the scriptures, the manuals,
And You and I took a walk.

The rich soil
The wise whispering trees
The birds
The glorious sunlight!

Then
A magical mist
And the gift of vibrant rejuvenation.

I learned so much!

My classroom is now
The wind
The light
The bird in flight
And the wisdom
Of delighting
In a rainbow.

IN THE RIVER

For many people this is a weekend playground.
But, for me, this river is sacred.

My hand dips carefully into the gently rushing waters
rising with a cup of gloriously glistening Bliss
that then pours onto my head,
dripping down,
across my wide-open eyes,
over my gleeful body,
and eventually back to the river.

I know with crystal clear certainty
that You are here.

I bathe myself in that certainty.
I pray to live fully in sync with that conviction.

A boat passes by with a sputtering motor.
A blue jay swoops overhead.
Across, on the other bank, children play and laugh
and a dog barks.

They're all oblivious to me,
the odd one in the water,
as I let myself get lost in a playful ritual,
diving into the mystical moment.

With free-flowing abandon I swim in Your Love.

This river is sacred.

TALKING OUT LOUD

Today, on a bench at the serene college campus
I was talking with You about patience and Love.
I brought my hands together, bowed my head and exclaimed loudly:
"Thank you!"

I looked up with a big, grateful grin on my face
and there, walking right in front of me,
was an anxious woman and a small child.

The woman nervously looked away.
I can't blame her -
a scruffy character alone on a bench talking loudly to himself
can be scary.

But the little girl wasn't frightened.
She stopped,
smiled brightly,
looked me in the eyes,
and waved.

She knew who I was talking to, didn't she?

I brought my hands together again and whispered softly
"Thank You."

VI

SIX

DANCE LESSONS

Dear One,

It's a strange exercise – this dance of being a spiritual human.

One moment I am bathed in light and Love
flowing with Your Grace.

Then, my nose itches.

And by the time I reach to scratch it,
my mind is off and running on other trivial tasks -
as if the majesty of Your Love was just a passing breeze.

Sometimes though,
more and more frequently,
by virtue of practice,
I can scratch the itch and still stay fully aware of Your Presence.

Thank you for dancing with me!

Thank You for Your Love -
ever-present -
whether I'm in step or not.

LAY IT DOWN

You say:

"It's going to be easier to walk with me
if you let go of what you're carrying."

"Lay it down."

"If you really want it or need it,
you can come back for it later."

Then on we go
free and easy.

YOUR REFLECTION

Walking past a bird sanctuary,
with its luscious wetlands,
I turn my head
and see the vast sky
reflected in the water.

No wonder the birds are so comfortable there!

Then,
suddenly,
in that moment,
I see Your reflection
in everything around me.

I can feel your Love flowing through it all.

No wonder I'm so comfortable here.

MAGIC CARPET

This old rug
beautiful and worn
where
I meditate
and pray
is a magic carpet

I sit on it
and
fly
to
You

FLYING

Flying in an airplane
over the land of my birth.

What an interesting trip this life has been!

Below me I see the patches of earth
carved into rectangles, squares, and circles
of green, brown, and blue.

At one time I thought I wanted and needed
to own one of those patches.

Now of course I am free to simply fly over them all,
appreciating their beauty and usefulness,
but knowing,
serenely,
that all I truly want and need
is You.

WATER

On the beach, the sea stretched before me sumptuously -
beautiful beyond all boundaries.

Later, the glass with ice was so refreshing.
The hot shower was so relaxing and nurturing.

I stopped to thank You for these vital nurturing gifts.
As I prayed, I looked down at my hands
They reminded me that,
like the sea, the ice, and the bath,
my body, too, is composed mostly of water.

Your Love
appearing as water
permeates everything.

When I
look out at the vast ocean,
float down the river,
or take a walk in the rain,
I can hear You say
"I Am Here."

You quench the deepest thirst of my Soul.

SECRET AGENT

I've never been one for espionage.
The whole thing seems so sneaky and dangerous.
Yet often I find myself working as a secret agent for You.

I generally don't talk about that job.
I just show up,
get the encrypted messages from Central Office,
then proceed with the assignment.

The messages are often coded in undetectable simplicity:

"Go for a walk now"
"Call that friend"
"Say hello to that stranger"

My special training empowers me
to intuitively decipher the instructions
and follow them
with stealth and subtlety.

Each assignment involves preparation and undercover work -
perhaps some prayers,
a helping hand,
a sincere smile,
or a few kind words,
at the right time
to the right person.

Funny though,
the mission is always the same:
Spread Love.

BLOWN AWAY

Your Divine Love
blew my mind again -

my tiny brain
exploding across the sky.

Now my empty head
can gaze serenely at the
infinite
sparkling
lights
above.

STEVER'S PRAYER

Thank You for another day.

Please guide me, help me, be with me.
You are my sweet Beloved, as I am Yours.

Thank You for watching over all the wonderful people in my life.

Please forgive my trespasses, judgments, resentments,
weaknesses, and mistakes,
as I forgive those of others.

Thank You for my strength, creativity,
compassion, kindness and Love.
Let's do more of that together!

May Your Light and Love be in every layer,
portion,
pore,
cell,
molecule,
atom,
particle of my being -
glowing and radiating forth -
healing, directing, energizing, informing, and transforming
this humble temporary vehicle
into an ever-better instrument of
Your Love.

VII

SEVEN

RESENTMENTS

Dear One,

There I go again, collecting resentments.

She said that.
He did this.
They don't… whatever.

How easily I collect these judgments.

I carry them around
like a heavy collection of broken bricks,
or a bag of dirty old clothes that no longer fit.

Then I look up at You
and I see Your light
shining on us All -
Your Love there for everyone.

When I let go of the self-absorbed burden
I'm free
to play
with joy
and wonder
in Your beautiful world.

MOVING

I am moving to a different home down the road.
Thank you for this opportunity!

I'm packing all my stuff - the sacred and the mundane.
Holy books and prayer beads, socks and toothbrushes.

We've done this many, many times,
You and I,
in this life and others.

Place to place
Room to room
Role to role

There's always a new adventure
and usually a few surprises.

I can relax and enjoy the journey,
knowing You are with me.

HOME

In the hot and windy desert,
hundreds of miles from my apartment,
on a borrowed blanket,
praying to You,

I look around and feel completely at home.

How can that be?
This is a strange and foreign place to me, but You are here.

You Are Here!

Your Presence is all I need to belong.

Any where.
Any way.
Any time.

Wherever You are,
I am home.

Lost in Love,
I am Home.

KEYS

Where are my f***ing keys!?!

I do this all the time,
frantically looking for something I desperately need.

I know it's somewhere,
but fail to notice that it's right here.

As it turns out…
The glasses were on top of my head.
The cellphone was in my bag.

Oh, of course, the keys are in my pocket.
They were right here all along.

I play this same game with You.
Restlessly I search.

Maybe You're online,
or in that new book,
or perhaps at that holy vacation destination.

But, You were right here all along.

From now on
Every time I think I need to search for You,
I will repeat this mantra:

The keys are in my pocket
The keys are in my pocket
The keys are in my pocket

The Beloved is in my heart
The Beloved is in my heart
The Beloved is in my heart

You are right here,
Always.

AFFIRMATION

Dear One,

I know that You are with me always
but sometimes I need a little help
to feel fully surrounded by Your Presence.

That's when I do this affirmation:

Love is underneath me.
Love is above me.
Love is to the left of me.
Love is to the right of me.
Love is behind me.
Love is in front of me.

Your Love
is within me
and around me
Always.

TEA PARTY

Feeling the kind of desolate fatigue
that's suited only for sitting quietly,
I pour a cup of tea and close my eyes.

You are here!
So I get up, and pour a cup of tea for You too,
and set it on the counter beside me.

There we sit, You and I,
Your vast Presence quietly comforting me.

Nothing to do, but be with You, as we sip our tea.

Eventually, as I see the scene before me,
my simple smile widens to a big grin.
How funny this might look to someone!
Here I am, an apparently mature and fully functioning adult,
sitting alone, in the kitchen, having a magical tea party with God.

As I chuckle at my childishness
it becomes obvious that You've done it again -
my empty tiredness has been transformed into relaxed delight.

How I Love hanging out with You!

I'll pour more tea and offer You a cookie.

THE DOER

There I was singing Your name and praises.
The thought came:
"What am I supposed to do to serve You?
Please tell me what to do!"

You said:
"Truly Love me. I will do the rest."

Yes!
Thank You.

You are the Doer.
I am the instrument.

CAPACITY

Dear One,

Maybe it's a good thing that, often, I forget who I truly am
and get pulled away from awareness of Your Presence.

Otherwise, I might get ungrounded
and take in more Light than I can handle right now.

Step by step I'm learning.

A steady and determined runner can train to go for miles.

A tiny seedling, barely able to stand the sun's intensity,
can grow into a tree that stretches gloriously to the light,
while housing birds and bearing fruit for us all.

A yogi, through diligent practice,
can eventually hold any pose,
and be consistently in awareness of You
while serving in the world with a quiet mind
and vastness of heart.

Okay. I'll keep working on it, striving to expand my capacity
until I am able to consciously be in Your Presence always.

You are at my side,
my divine coach,
Lovingly pushing me to the limit
but never giving me more than I am ready for.

All for Love.

HIBISCUS

Walking with You
late one afternoon,
running my fingers along a metal fence.

On the other side of the fence is a row of
Brightly blooming yellow hibiscus flowers.

Behind the hibiscus is a manicured complex of
elegant condominium homes.
It costs millions of dollars to live in one of those houses.

The hibiscus are all reaching out,
away from the condos towards the sidewalk -
Pushing through, above, and beyond the fence
To the sunlight.

I pause, and the flowers and I have a chat
About how blessed we are.

VIII

EIGHT

STORM

Dear One,

So much drama!

Raucous rain,
thunder,
lightening,
and wind
in viciously tumultuous gusts

The air and ground
overwhelmed and battered
with wild wet havoc.

It was terrifying!

The electricity went out.

But the Sun
the Moon
and
You
were in place,
steady and calm,
as always,
through it all.

You are with me during all my storms.

JUSTICE

Walking down the street,
angry about injustice -
righteously upset about
the pain and suffering people cause others.

So much hurt and misery.
What can I do?

I ask:
Where's the Love in this?

You say:
I am Here.

I ask:
What can I do?
What can Love do?

The answer comes:
Love can act through me
if I stay connected to the Presence.

I can fiercely fight for justice with an Open Heart.

So I pray some more,
pick a doable corner of the complex of problems,
draw a line in the sand,
and get to work.

Love in Action can change the world.

TUNING STRINGS

Dear One,

I know that my body, mind, and life are here
for You to use as you wish,

just like a brilliant musician uses their instrument,
perhaps a violin or guitar,
to create beauty and inspire us.

I pray every day for You to use me
as an instrument
of your peace and Love.

But I get so lazy about tuning the strings,
slow to do the things
that keep me fit and ready for your flow.

Please grant me the strength, self-discipline, and energy
to make the adjustments needed
for my mind,
body,
and spirit
to be useful to You.

STUDENT LOANS

Dear One,

I used to be a good student,
what they call "smart."

I always did well on tests and trivia games.

I received all sorts of academic degrees, licenses, and certificates.

Then I started hanging out with You.

Now,
all I know
is Love.

But I still have to pay for all those student loans.

MIRROR

Thank You for using me to help others.

When I walk with You,
and live from my heart,
Your Love transforms me
into a subtle mirror.

Reflecting a person's Soul
back to them,
so their mind can see it.

Their mind doesn't always know that it's You doing the work.

But our Souls recognize each other instantly.

LET IT GO

Dear One,

I got a little lost today.

I didn't even notice
that I was pursuing negative feelings and empty desires,
getting trapped
in dead end thoughts.

As it always does, that foolish game got complicated,
disappointing,
confusing,
and exhausting.

In the meantime, I'd lost focus on You.

So there I sat,
in the park,
on this beautiful sunny day,
feeling miserable.

How ridiculous!

So I took a deep breath,
and spoke Your name.

Now
You
are Here.

I can feel Your Love all around me.

A soft warm breeze blows through me
as You gently say:

"Let it go, let it go, let it go"

I smile.

Every cell of my being relaxes.

I let go.

Your Love is all I need.

LITTLE HOUSE

I live in a little house with my friend.
Now that You've moved in,
we talk more and more about the Great Love.

It's as if You, me, and my friend are married.

Each of us goes out each day,
into the world,
doing our best.

Then we trek home,
helping ourselves, and each other,
to Your bounty.

Cooking, cleaning, sleeping,
meditating,
praying,
dancing
and singing

Reaching into each delicious moment -
extraordinarily
delightfully
divinely
vibrating
in Love.

BAKING BREAD

Here I am, on a casual, chilly day, baking bread.
It smells so heavenly!

I remember my mom cheerfully baking bread, now and then,
as did my sister, my aunt, my grandmother
and countless generations of bakers before them.

Somehow, I feel them all close to me right now.
They gather around as I pull the magic loaf out of the oven.

And of course, You are here,
just as You've always been,
during the humble creation of every loaf.

Ahhhh, this warm, fresh miracle is so delicious
and the taste is truly divine.

PLANTING A TREE

What's the difference
between saying a prayer
and planting a tree?

Nothing, if the intention is the same.

When I chat with a tree
the conversation
is always about You
and the joy
of reaching
towards the Light.

IX

NINE

THE CATERER

I used to work as a caterer -
planning, preparing, and serving fancy food
on beautiful plates in amazing places
for important special events.

Everything had to be perfect or the client would be upset.
My reputation, business, and livelihood were always on the line.

Now I serve only You,
in all I do.

I still strive for a gentle perfection,
but when I fall short,
as I often do,
You never get upset.

You never complain, judge, or criticize.
You just keep on Loving me.

You are the ultimate client, and this job pays extremely well.

Thanks for hiring me to serve You!

My resume now is Love.

HOME IN THE CITY

Dear One,

City life can be so chaotic!

Walking through the crowded dirty streets today
I almost stepped in dog shit.
Loud sirens whizzed by
and in the next block
I was nearly hit by a car.

Then I decided to stop and buy a flower
I made it to my block
stepped into my building
and into my apartment.

I put the flower on my altar.
In order to calm down from the bustle and near accident
I sat to pray and meditate for a moment.
I took a breath and gazed at the flower
saw Your beauty
and felt Your Love in my heart.

I dwell within this chaotic city.
In the middle of this city is my home.
Sitting in that home is my fragile body and beating heart.
In the center of the heart dwells a tiny flower.
In the center of that flower dwells the entire universe - Your Love

A MIRACLE

While praying and singing your praises,
I selfishly asked for a miracle.

You said,
"Stop praying and stop Loving me and I'll give you a miracle."

I said,
"No way! I will never give up our Love for anything."

You said,
"There's your miracle."

Thank You.

HIDE AND SEEK

Strolling home I playfully ask,
"What is Love up to today?"

I take a breath and wait for Your Presence.

And I wait some more…
Where are You?

Then I catch a glimpse:

You're hiding
in the breeze
in the blossoming tree
in the perfection of the perfection of a bird in flight
in that child's grin.

Oh wow!
You're hiding in every
face,
every tree,
every flower.
You are everywhere.

What fun games we play!

FOREST PRAYER

Your greenery cloaks and comforts me
Your earth supports me
Your water enlivens me
Your air, it lifts me
Your Light
Is my Light
Thank You

SILENCE

I sat alone on the hill
with no intention other than to be there
quietly
for a little while.

Resting in front of me
was a large stone
from an ancient lava flow.

There we sat
the stone and I

Two lumps of matter
both made by You.

In that silence
reality began to widen
like the sky at sunrise

And I saw that the stone was secretly still on fire
glowingly sharing its story with me
as I melted ever further
into the
endless
silent
moment
of Your Presence.

HARMONY

Chanting ancient prayers
and singing Your names
with my dear friend
from a distant country

He noticed
that when we say
these sacred prayers together
we are speaking the same language

In beautiful, natural harmony
just as we were meant to do.

No borders
No boundaries

Two souls
fulfilling their true purpose -

Channeling Your Love.

BOWL OF LOVE

Dear One,

Sometimes I eat snacks and sweets voraciously
as if they're going to fulfill me.

Tonight I think I'll skip that bowl of ice cream
choosing instead
to take a walk
and feast
on Your Presence.

Treats are fine now and then,
but they're poor replacements for the joy and nourishment
of a spiritual banquet.

Your Love is all the sweetness I need.

EVERYTHING CHANGED

Walking home through the city streets
on this gray day
my mind was dull;
my attention vague and gloomy.

Then it came -
a soft gentle rain.

I noticed.

Then everything changed!

The fragrance was delightful -
and I instantly recognized that it was You.

"You're here!" I whispered,
and all the colors came alive.

As the drizzle became a shower
every drop sang Your name.

I let myself get gloriously soaked.

X

TEN

BEAUTIFUL

This afternoon, feeling weak and disheveled,
I found myself at a golf course, of all places,
and sat down by the lake.

A beautiful white egret strolled past me
then took off,
sailing inches above the water.

From there, she soared
with astounding grace and ease
into Your vast sky

Where,
at some point,
everything blossoms
into everything else.

I sat by the lake
and, for that moment,
I, too, soared
and felt
serenely
Beautiful.

IN THE COLD

Walking home just now,
on this painfully cold and wet January night
I was singing.

And thought to myself:
"It's a good day
I believe in Love"

Wow! What happened to the grumpy me?
The part that says "Winter sucks?"

I must be doing something right,
all because of You.

TOURISM

Working on travel plans: reservations, flights, and hotels.

As I take a break to sense Your Presence,
I'm reminded that I'm always a tourist in this world.

Throughout this lifetime I'm just visiting for a while,
going here and there,
checking out the sites,
enjoying the locals, the food, the attractions -
trying to thoroughly enjoy the trip
and all of the interesting experiences.

Then,
eventually,
one way or another,
it's time
to
go
back
home
to
You.

STORAGE UNIT 28

For so many years I've paid rent
on a container filled with stuff.

Stuff I once used,
stuff I thought I might use again,
books I'd already read,
clothes that no longer fit,
abandoned appliances,
and some dusty holiday decorations.

Sometimes I'd go there to take stuff out,
perhaps an old stool.
Or I'd put stuff in,
perhaps an old lamp.

Yeah, I might need my high school yearbooks
for something important down the road.

And those old paintings might start looking attractive some day.

And how about those tools I once used
for fixing the house I no longer have?

All this stuff -
buckets and shovels for building castles in the sand.

And, in the corner,
a box of photos of those castles -
pictures taken before the waves washed them away.

Why did I think I needed all that stuff,
when all I ever really wanted or needed was You?

It took several days of work to sort through
and get rid of all that useless weight.

Storage unit 28 is now empty.

They're sending me my deposit.

I think I'll spend it on flowers
to place on the altar where I meditate and pray.

A gift for You.

I'll be amazed by their intricate beauty
every day
until they wither and fade
making way
for another moment
with You.

TEACHERS

Dear One,

I'm so thankful for all the teachers in my life!

The wise, the glowing, the generous, the gracious,
and also the assholes.

Er… I mean,
Thank You as well for the challenging things people say and do.
Through their negative words and actions,
and the trail of pain they cause,
I learn to avoid the same path
and strive to be more Loving and considerate.

In your Light, everyone I meet is a teacher -
an opportunity to practice kindness and Love.

Ah, but I humbly admit
that I'm especially grateful for the
glistening
golden
Souls -
those teachers that are clearly connected to You.

The ones whose footsteps I try to follow.

Where would I be without them?

PAUSE

Dear One,

There it is again,
Your soothing whisper,
inviting me to pause.

I remember the first time I heard it, many years ago.

My dog had just died,
I was taking care of my elderly dad,
I was sick,
and work was crazy.

At one point I was so overwhelmed,
from so many angles,
that I began spinning out of control.

Your message brought me safely into the moment.
Ahhhh…

Since then, when I forget, You remind me.

I may be anxious, or resentful, or craving, or just too busy.
Then I hear You and follow Your simple suggestion:

"Why not pause for a moment and focus on Love?"

CIRCLE

Today I sat in a circle of friends
singing your praises for hours.

Among us was a young baby
who was very fussy when she and her mother first arrived.
But as soon as we started singing
she became calm and remained blissful for the entire three hours.

The energy in the room was so high and vibrant -
full of light and Love.

I imagined the baby's Soul saying:
"Ah, this is what I came to this life *for*,
and this is what I came *from*."

Right now, as I tell you this, I realize that's true for me, too.

Your Love is what I came for
And Your Love is what I came from.

UNDER THE BLANKET

What a transformative gathering we just had!
Thank You for bringing us all together
under Your blanket of Love.

So many people
from so many different places and backgrounds.
So many roles to play:
mother, father, partner, child,
teacher, student, musician, doctor, poet, clerk,
loud, quiet, lost, found...

But here we meet as kindred Souls.
Souls on a journey to You.

One Soul says that by Your Grace
we wander here in time and space
called to the unexpected miracle.

Another Soul says they didn't even know
that such unconditional Love exists.
They didn't know
that Your Love was patiently waiting for them.

Your Love
Flowing through us
Heart to Heart
Soul to Soul

Under Your blanket all things are possible.

PIZZA

Full moon
on a warm tropical night.

We took a walk
ordered a pizza
and sat outside -
talking about Your Love.

Your Love
freshly baked
into the moment!

I took a bite.

Nothing could be more delicious.

XI

ELEVEN

SLAP IN THE FACE

When I first got the diagnosis
it felt like a slap in the face.

Then, over time,
I came to see it as a nudge -
A gracious push
to turn my gaze toward You.

You -
the source of my Joy,
my true reason to live.

When the clamor and commotion of life
suck up all my time and energy,
clogging my days so much
that Love is obscured

Something always happens
to remind me of
You.

In Your arms I rest and heal.

IN THE CORNER

I am sitting
in the corner of the room
On the floor
late at night
with a grin

The only sound
is the faint hum
of the refrigerator in the kitchen

The noise and worries of the day have gone to bed
leaving me to marvel
at the candlelight dancing on the wall
while I rub my feet on the beautiful old rug
and lay back on the big gold pillow

Tonight, this corner is a discrete little piece of Heaven -
A gift You left for me to discover
at a time just like this

I think I'll put this treasure in my pocket
and carry it with me into the morning

Tomorrow, when I go about the tasks of the day
conducting transactions and chatting about the weather
no one will know
about this precious moment
I have tucked away

But they may wonder about my grin.

FIRE

Overnight the fire raged through the old town,
close to my house,
ravaging everything it could.

Lives devastated.
Lives lost.
So much suffering and pain.

I don't understand why these things happen.

I don't understand why my place was spared.

I don't understand Your part in this.

But I do understand,
without a doubt,
my part in this.

My role is to Love and serve,
as best I can.

Please grant me knowledge of how I can help,
and the strength to carry that out.

TIME TO GO HOME

In the middle of a stressful work day
I leave to take a walk.

Maybe with a few minutes outside I can figure it out:
What should I do about that project?
How should I deal with that negative coworker?
When should I… on and on.

So much to do
So much on my mind
So overwhelming!

Then I remember
to stop
and talk
to You.

You say:
"It's time to come home."

I say:
"I can't go home, I've got to go back to work and…"

You say
again
gently but clearly
"It's time to come home."

Then I get it.

The message is:
It's time
to come home
to the Heart.

All it takes
is to pause everything
for just a moment
and focus on Love.

So I take a deep breath
and feel
Your Presence.

From there life flows sweetly.

When I stop thinking about the situations of the day
and
rest
in
Your
Love
everything
falls
into
place.

CHILDREN AT SUNSET

Walking with You at dusk,
breathing in the air and light,
I pass by a gaggle of young kids
as they play, yell, and laugh -
delightfully absorbed in their games.

Then a dad comes out and says it's time to come in.
A mom opens a door to shout that dinner is ready.

So it is with You and me.

Some of Your children have to be reminded,
almost every night,
that it's time to stop playing and come in to rest.

It's sometimes difficult to stop the games and playful fantasies,
but the peace and nourishment You offer is what energizes it all.

Your nurturing Love makes playtime possible.

CELEBRATION

The evening sky was gray as I sat on the porch thinking:
"Oh, time to check my emails."

Then happy music came drifting up the street,
urging me into the moment.

Just then - Bam! – the sundown sky burst
into a most glorious and extravagant banquet of color.

Wow!

I walked through the grass, beneath your light show,
to see what the music was about.

It was a celebration -
for drug addicts graduating from rehab!

Such a blessed event -
lives renewed and ready to blossom
under Your magnificent Light.

The spectacular sunset
announced a new dawn for them,
and a festive renewal for all of us.

You sure do throw a great party!

THE SWIMSUIT

Oh, Beloved, I must've been crazy.
I nearly said no to a night swim!
My shyness almost kept me away.
Instead, I somehow came to my senses and said Yes.

Somebody loaned me a swimsuit from their pile of trunks.
The four of us walked or wheeled through the dark
and into the water.

We looked up
and there You were
in all Your magnificence!

So many stars… stretching our minds,
pulling on every cell in our bodies
to join them.

Surrounded and held by the warm water,
somebody said that You arrange and rule all that infinite Light.

Somebody else said that when You open Your mouth
all those stars could be seen inside your being.

Somebody said that it is written
that You live deep in our hearts.

Somebody noticed that, like stars,
each of us is made of tiny particles,
skillfully gathered together for a moment in time.

There we were, specks of Light
gazing blissfully at Your ocean of stars.

In that moment we touched Oneness.

I kept the swimsuit as a souvenir.

Tonight, a week later, folding laundry,
I came upon the swim trunks,
with their faded Hawaiian print.

I clutched them to my heart
as if they were a precious sacred relic.

Perhaps they are.

SHAMPOO

Taking a shower tonight,
I reached behind the disorderly row
of favorite soaps and conditioners
for a bottle of shampoo I seldom use.

One morning,
several weeks ago,
I'd been praying before I bathed,
and it was with a deep feeling
of Your Presence
that I had washed my hair
using this same, often disregarded, shampoo.

It was a simple but sacred cleansing.

Tonight,
pouring a bit of the creamy liquid onto my hand
and lifting it to my head,
a whiff of the fragrance
took me instantly back
to that past moment of bliss.

Then,
just as quickly as the scent had transported me
to that prayerful morning,
I found myself back in tonight's shower,
but fully reconnected to that past feeling
of Divine Presence.

That moment became this moment.

Drying off,
talking to You,
and writing this down,
I continue to feel
Your Love
in every pore of my being.

It seems that we stash
these subtle memos for ourselves
everywhere
Sometimes on purpose.
Sometimes unknowingly.

The idea is that,
eventually,
everything becomes a reminder.

Then we'll no longer need the little prompts.

We can just be in Your Presence all the time.

We can just Be Love.

HEARTBEAT

Dear One,

My heart works so earnestly
Pumping life through me
Steady as a clock.

Mostly I don't hear it
But sometimes
In a gentle quiet night
When I am falling asleep
There it is
A faint drumbeat.

As I listen
I can also feel
My Spiritual heart beating

Every thump
Making a gentle vibration
Like a drop of water
Into an endless sea

Ever so slowly rippling out
Until, eventually, waves form
And the precious Love
Flows unbounded
To distant shores.

XII

TWELVE

THE GRAND PRIZE

Once so fast and deliberate,
my steps are slowing down.

I tell my body and loyal feet -
It's okay, slowdown if you must.

But my heart…

I pray that my heart will continue its inspired pace.

I pray that I can continue to Love
in glorious abandon
with as much depth
and flowery brilliance
as my Soul can channel!

For that Love is the true gift of life -
The Grand Prize!

And the only way to claim it is to
Love
Love
Love!

Showing You
and the world
how grateful I am.

FREE

At sunset,
I leaned back against a tree
And let earthly strength
hold the cumbersome weight of my body.

I took a deep breath
into my Heart
And let You
carry the luminous weight of my Soul.

A gentle breeze passed by
to tell me
I am free…

I am free
I am free
I am free

SLEEPY

Sometimes when I am sleepy
not yet in bed
but my tasks are done
and the day is spent

I sit quietly
with the companionship of a book
whose pages offer
a tempting late-night nibble
of spiritual delights
that I am too drowsy to absorb.

So I just sit there with my book
And feel Your Loving arms around me -
so comforting
strong,
gentle,
and real
that there's nothing
I have to do
but be sleepy.

Nothing I have to do
but Be.

FROM THE JUNGLE

I hope You got the message that we sent You tonight
from that place in the jungle.

Friends meditating, our discussion turned into a prayer.

We were trying to say:
The path to You is beautiful, glorious,
and the soul reason we're here.

We were trying to say:
We are beginning to see that the tools of the path
are also the signposts and the destination –
Forgiveness
Compassion
Love
Love
Love.

I'm sorry if our words were clumsy, awkward, unfocused.
Our voices faltered, but our eyes…
Our eyes.

We could clearly *see* what we were trying to say
in each other's eyes.

We could clearly see You
in each other's eyes.

EXHALED

They lovingly washed his body
And laid it out
Dressed in white
With flowers all around

It was beautiful

But he was no longer there
No longer confined by physical limits
He's with You now
Boundlessly

His presence
Flows into Your Presence
Which flows everywhere

Like a deep breath
Gently
Exhaled
Into the vast sky

On an exquisitely perfect day.

BREATHING

I sat there
thinking of You -

breathing
in
Your
Presence.

I let
my
self
get lost.

Then, suddenly,
the layers of pretense were gone.

It was just You and me
as the same thing.

Just Love.

STEVER'S MOTTO

LOVE

As much as you can,

From where you are,

With what you've got.

ALL FOR THIS

And in the end it was all for this -

To stand peacefully in Your Presence
watching the light
dancing
on
the
endless
flow
of
waves

THANK YOU

ABOUT THE AUTHOR

Steven "Stever" Dallmann PhD is a spiritual practitioner, writer, teacher, and licensed psychotherapist.

In 2008 he founded the non-profit Liberation Institute in San Francisco, a community organization with an innovative model of offering mental health services to the entire community regardless of income.

Stever currently resides and practices on the island of Maui in Hawaii, from where he continues to guide the ever-expanding Liberation Institute, and is deeply involved in Hanuman Maui (The Ram Dass Loving Awareness Sanctuary), Aloha in Action, and various community and writing projects.

Learn more at steverdallmann.com

www.ingramcontent.com/pod-product-compliance
Lightning Source LLC
Chambersburg PA
CBHW030303130626
46549CB00002B/673